About the Author

The real goal of poetry, maybe even of writing in general, is meeting oneself. Through the other, through the others, through the decisions one makes, the choices whose consequences are sometimes painful yet instructive, through intense experiences of emotions, what one looks for and finds is oneself. Naomi B. endlessly tests her limits, plays with her heart and her body, and remains fascinated, curious, optimistic, and alive. If she is, it is partly because her projects are multiple, young, old, and strong. She clings to them. They cling to her, too. Writing is the mark she will leave off her resilience.

Cycle

Naomi B.

Cycle

Olympia Publishers
London

www.olympiapublishers.com
OLYMPIA PAPERBACK EDITION

Copyright © Naomi B. 2024

The right of Naomi B. to be identified as author of
this work has been asserted in accordance with sections 77 and 78 of
the Copyright, Designs and Patents Act 1988.

All Rights Reserved

No reproduction, copy or transmission of this publication
may be made without written permission.
No paragraph of this publication may be reproduced,
copied or transmitted save with the written permission of the publisher,
or in accordance with the provisions
of the Copyright Act 1956 (as amended).

Any person who commits any unauthorised act in relation to
this publication may be liable to criminal
prosecution and civil claims for damage.

A CIP catalogue record for this title is
available from the British Library.

ISBN: 978-1-80439-951-4

This is a work of fiction.
Names, characters, places and incidents originate from the writer's imagination. Any resemblance to actual persons, living or dead, is purely coincidental.

First Published in 2024

Olympia Publishers
Tallis House
2 Tallis Street
London
EC4Y 0AB

Printed in Great Britain

Dedication

I dedicate this collection to my sisters, Kenza and Maïlys, who are two jewels in my life.

Acknowledgements

Thank you everyone who read my first poetry collection, *Gold*. Thanks to you, I have felt recognition and *Cycle* could be published. There is nothing like the feeling of being heard and seen, nothing like being told your emotions have been acknowledged. Thank you everyone who allowed me to make myself and *Gold* a bit more known. Thank you for displaying my book on a shelf in your shop, for accepting my advertising, for listening to me read my poems out loud, for congratulating me, for taking a look at a copy on a short visit to a bookstore or a book festival, for sharing feedback with me after you read the collection, for asking for a signature, for encouraging me. Thank you, Inès. You were, just like for *Gold*, the very first reader of this collection. Thank you, Alex. You are not in this collection, but you will be with me always. Thank you, all the souls who people my world. Thank you for your smiles, support, honesty, kindness and humour. Thank you, Maman and Papa. Thank you, Kenza and Maïlys. As always. And forever.

DAZZLED

She said,
you're still looking
for yourself—

I said,
that's not true.

I've been to Sweden,
and didn't find her

I've been to England,
and couldn't see her

I've been to Ireland
but she flew away

I've been to Scotland,
where she stayed away

I've been to Italy,
and caught a glimpse of her

To my abandoned land,
and smelled and brushed her

I've come back home,
but she had gone again—

It's only when I
met your eyes
that I saw her,
her silhouette,
her skin colour
It's only when I
heard your voice
that I heard her,
and she whispered words that I traced with ink—

I know nothing of your world—

Like travelling memories
Blow pictures into my mind—

My body is an eel

Undulating on your flesh-made wall

Squeaking when your promise-made hands

Travel on my scales—

Wet lips and greedy tongue—

                                  I knew
                           Before licking
                      That your flavour was

                  Nectar—

—echoing tears

Your past sufferings
Sticking to
Your skin
Your flesh
Like old wounds
Loving you to death—

They are pebbles
Rebounding onto
My skin
My flesh
Like new wounds
For I love you to death.

If you could hear
the blood running
to my heart
flowing—

If you could meet with the clouds I have in
mind—

You've passed the threshold.

You've liked the hall.

Will you love
The dungeons, the cells
The secret passageways—

Overwhelming
The world is
People and rhyming words—

And I feel choked
Delightfully
By the music that you make—

They sing for me—
The things she keeps in mind for me
The things she thinks she must tell me
Ask me
The words that take shape in her mind
The process of it—before they take the shape of thoughts
—the assemblage of words—

I'm a thinker
In love with
And in need of
Someone else's thinking process.

LOVE
a thick, greyish-pinkish
smoke
that invades your body
takes control of your mind
of the
strongest
most stubborn
parts of you—
and yet

LOVE
makes you
lean to
it, ask
for more
it's like that
smoke
in theme parks or fairs
that smells like
candyfloss
—surprise
—love it
—invading
—gone
—miss—

LOVE
candyfloss smoke

It's a boomerang thing
A ricochet thing
A basketball—bouncing—

Your sadness

From A to B—
From you to me—

—LION EYES

Look—
It isn't only I who see
you
as
 a divinity
The angels up there
knotted a thread
to the right corners of your eyes.
And they pull up—pull up—
with their fairy-like strength—

One day I looked up—
no angel—
and no sun
And when I looked back down
the angels
had put the sun in your eyes

I thought honey
I thought hazel
Caramel
I thought skin
and I thought gold—

But when you turned
to me
I felt
Warmth—

And I wondered
what is the sun in your eyes
saw in me

How can the sun be?
interested in the breeze?

When you breathed my hair
We made a creature out of our
backs and arms
the first time we held
in the dark—

The ground: *cotton candy*
around: blowing wind

Only your hands on my back
kept me from falling
down
from flying
away—

After holding you
I went to bed with an image—
hand-shaped marks on my skin.
Just like when
kids dive their moist, little hands
into paint
and mark the wall—

I dropped my heart at her feet
And she swallowed it
When we held
I felt it beating in our chest—

I have lived in our first kiss
Dropped my life on the tip of your tongue
And died on your upper lip—

My mouth is dry
For my head is a desert of words—

And your breath digs a path in me
And I listen to the notes you make
And I get lost in your oasis brain
And I pour myself a drink—
And then I sip peacefully.

Yet you might suffocate
In the heat of my unshared
Secrets—

See, I'm used to warmth and sweat
To silence—loneliness

Words
  are rivers under my pen—
But canyons of emptiness
  on my tongue, thick breath—

Yet I promise to learn
The swimming to wateriness
The steps to openness
To quench your thirst
To not lose your hand in the
Desert of my brain—

You took your seat next to my makers
For you have made a part of me

In my head, a seed has grown
watered since January—

It has vanquished the cold
the rain and the snow
Summer and the blow—

In my head the seed proceeds
keeping on sipping—

And I can see petals now—
and perhaps very soon
a pretty flower bloom—

None of us holds a mirror—
Yet
My sex my belly my breasts
Sing back to
Your sex your belly your breasts.

There aren't enough hands of yours
There isn't enough skin
There aren't enough hands
to hold me
to stroke me
There aren't enough hands
on me
in me
There isn't enough you
for me—

Grow an extra hand or two
So that you
Can take *full* possession of
My body—

You make me rain between my legs
You make me salivate—

My body is the map you' ve been travelling in
You used your fingers to find your path
And easily got lost on my riverbanks—
My body is the map you' ve been travelling in
You used your fingers to find your path
And easily got lost on my riverbanks—

We left and were left off
Like heavy bags on the way
To carry each other
On a lighter pathway

Love is a trade-off
a bright feeling
so
beaming
it makes you pay
the most expensive price
to set a balance in
your emotional system

I wish I could steal and run away—

Love is such
an amazing
empowering
melting
overwhelming
weakening
feeling—

I wish there wasn't
that shadow
frustration
obsession
concussion
un - ex - plain - a - ble

emotion—

For they destroy the soul
and always win the fight against

Reason
—that silent battle—
They end up
R. U. L. I. N. G
over your best decision—

BLIND

I feel a Funeral
in my chest—

My love for you is too heavy
Our arms are struggling, shaking—

My love is a hundred years old
We might be too young still—

You spread an air of hope
I blow the words of love

You turn your back on me

I paint with my fingers
The words of love again

On your back—

It seems that you can't feel

Anything—

Cursed love curses

I let the robbers in
Rolled out the red carpet for them

First
They robbed me in the place of Light
Then
In the place of Warmth—

I was left with nothing but
Pictures of what I'd lost
Tears
And rooms to fill

You spat the word
Bandage

You would have been a bandage

Let me be the bandage
What a privilege
To cover your wound
What is pride?
What is self-love?
Self-respect
When I would have *shined* being
Your bandage

Farewell to Beauty:

I knew
When you look away
And mentioned honesty—I knew.

My arms warned me
Tingling like sparkles
And I started to
Memorize the scars on your skin.

Yet I know—
Though I cried in your arms

Yet I know

I know I'll survive.

Yet I know—

No more pounding in my chest
My heart died—
My ribcage fell apart
I heard the bones crack—

I held my body
But I wanted *you* to hold me
Murderer and *comforter*
Of my frozen flesh—

And then I slid back
To nativity
Broke into pieces
In my parents' bellies—
They held what was left of me.

It is the memories
The promises
The hopes
The smells
The touch
The taste—
We are animals and
I'll miss...
Your tangibility

I chose love over hate
Peace, not contempt.

I told you go and don't look back

Heal and love yourself.

All the things I wanted you to know
All the things I wanted to tell you
And didn't have the time to
I'll die with them—
They're caterpillars that will rot in my chest—

At least I let a butterfly escape in a

                              you.
                      love
I

You expect smiles
a sweep
a bunch of
lies
and pretend—

But

I am not an actor
My heart glitters through my eyes
and paths of shed tears
are traced
memorized
on my social mask—

You ask for
the world
oblivion
when my stomach still squeaks with
shock
and disbelief—

I haven't brushed the bottom yet—
Let me take a glimpse of it

—it might have her scent—

Cheer up
No one needs to
witness
such
misery—

But

I am not an actor
My body's cold and shakes
and craves sleep—

I am a summer storm
I need to plunge
swim and drown
in my own wound
mourn the loss of my hopes—

So I can
rise
or
only a veil would cover
a bunch of old lies
and she'll still be
in my mind—

I'm a dreamer
I dreamed you
Making *poems* out of you—

I should have tried
To stay safe and sound
On the ground—
But I saw care in your eyes
And jumped into your hot-air balloon

I let myself fall into her arms
like a sigh
into the air—

Cycle

One year of you
I have lived an entire life
Loving you—

There are moments when you call out for all the strength of humanity—

Call out

For your ancestors' energy—

Christmas lights don't light up my world
Let me mourn my love
Turn Christmas carols into burial songs
Let me mourn alone

The girls I didn't like hearing about
you made me one of them—

I am a portrait among portraits—
Pale faces and streaming tears—

I felt
my sisters' disease—

The only comfort
an end can bring.

It's when night and silence slither in
That the weight of missing you creeps in
Like a bomb ticking
Counting
The seconds before exploding—

It's when peaceful quiet lures
That your voice in my head roars
And I'm left in here sinking—

I know now
it is your shell
that was moulded in
the same
iron
as mine—
What was underneath?
was a common
pain
and need for love—
We joined in an embrace
of tears wrinkled with age—

The armour
I had forged in
a lifetime
with
hundreds of layers
you
shot
and pierced it
a million holes to let your light in—
I
scratched your shell
but the last layer...
Too thick for my nails

I still
felt your heart
in our embrace

free

Where has this queen of reason gone
The one with reins over dotted frenzy
With a crown of silver on her forehead
Lighthouse that had never left me—

I used to rest on her wisdom
I used to follow her judgement blindly
Would believe in her imperious creeds
And now she has abandoned me—

"Oh, but *she* has never ruled"
A slithering voice whispered in me
"You know you' ve ignored her straight, white lines
Were fooled by some treachery—

Your true empress is a beat
Your blind, overruling enemy
Your mistress with whips and giant guards
A crown of gold and jewellery—

Others and you believed you pure
An incorruptible rock on the sea
Washed by the licking of the ruthless waves

But standing still as you should be—"

I shuddered at the voice's words
For I knew her eye had seen right through me
Until forgotten *pride* stroke in my chest
Resonating in my belly!

"You're wrong," I countered the voice
"I know you but you do not know me
My Will has power over us all
And my Will, will set me free—

I'll trip, won't know who to trust
For two queens, I will have loyalty
But I know over Reason and Heart
My Will, will have sovereignty."

Lost fifteen pounds
in seven days—

Did she weigh?
so heavy
in me?

Did trust and hope and dreams and love
counted
for so much
in my body?

Too much love to give
It makes ghosts appear—

Loneliness is a Spectre.

I don't remember
The first word
I learnt—

But I'll remember
The first and last ones
We gave each other—

It took me some courage to
Write the first word—

Then we formed a curl
With our words
And tongues—

Until we
Breathed each other's scent
For the very last time—
And drew farewell letters
On a teardrop wallpaper—

It's taking me courage to
Drop the pen—

Why is my life
Shaped
With silent music?

Why is writing so well
Laced
With courage?

It was the
unnatural cessation of it all
that orchestrated the final blow—

friendship

I'm taking down the Christmas tree
And all the Christmas lights
Like I'm taking down all the strength
I'd poured into our relationship.

the party's over

My forty-five-year-old friend had warned me—
One day—you'll see—
Your body won't be yours
But the representation
Of an expectation
A womb
A life-bearing machine—
You'll see
As soon as you reach the great age of thirty
Your breasts will be made of
Milk only—
You'll hear—and carry—
The hopes and disappointments and hurry
Of an entire family—
It was like this for me.

Yesterday
I wrote to my friend the words
They didn't wait for thirty.

Howling wind and tormented skies
Northern legends, rolling tempests—
He cried his rage to the unseen
At the top of some rugged hill—

Cursing, roaring but hurting beneath
—a pistol for the long unkissed cheek—
He threatened God, called out for spirits
Life could no longer be—

The haunting presence answered back
Taking the shape of a twisted tree
Together they dug a hole in the ground
Life could no longer be—

Someone made me taste company
and it was sweet—
Didn't have the bitterness
Of loneliness

In a blink, I clung to it
To the lips that delivered it—

When they stepped away I heard
The hoofs of looming death galloping to me
It was the aftertaste of solitude
Finding its way
Back—

And it was bitter—oh how bitter it was
For I had grown to love
The sugar on her lips—

No queen of reason—

No silver crown—

My true empress is a beat.

Searching for reasons
trying to understand
what it feels like to be in your mind
or as close as I can get—

Will I
see what you see in her
fall for what you've fallen for—
Will the triangle be?
a circle?

But though my efforts
are as hard as hard can be
though my heart beats for each of your beats

I do not
see.
I do not
fall.

What has she that others can't afford?

Is it I who is blind?
Or is your love
blinding you
or making you *see*—

I wished
I could have enveloped you with my words
Weaved you a second skin
A layer of love—a shield.

Now I wish
I could take my brain out for a minute and
Breathe.

How can you annihilate someone?
You've turned into a sun—

How can you take the sun down—?

Were they poisoned kisses?
Was there
Lethal elixir
In your saliva and breath—

Wouldn't I
Change my eyes
For her eyes
And see
Scenes one two three
Our staring, kissing, goodbyes
From her dearest, golden sight—

When my heart broke for the first time I thought

There—

It has met one of the pointiest fangs
Known one of the hardest flinches

There—

I' ve entered the land of
Second-hand pieces of beating flesh—

I felt the danger
But rushed to the end
Of the thread I'm
Tiptoeing backwards on

Cause you
Put an end
To my dance

Too much love to give—

I answer the call
Of a future lover's pain

Oh, why can't I find my horde?
And fly away with them
Like a dule of stooping doves—
I've been running after
the feeling of being loved
and wanted

Hold me love me want me
undress me in the end
and show me that I'm
worthy of what I've lost—

Solitude:

Whenever you leave me
Surrounded by other souls than mine
I seek your company—

Whenever we spend too much time together
I get sick of your invisibility
Your empty arms and soundless promises—
I'll reject you and beg
For my kind's company—

So many tos and fros—
Were we made for each other—?
Were you made to soothe my woes?
Or give me another—

Masks on our faces
Curtains on our tears
Lies over voices—

Why is it that we
Hold on to life
To *feel*
And hide away—frightened—
At the thought
The Other might see—

Are we strangers now?
Don't you recall my tastes?
My reading, writing, love interests—

Isn't
My flesh your flesh?
Our hearts and brains
The same?
Our pain—
Question yourself
Awake—
Was my crime to grow so great?

A day of inky toil—
Mind emptied—pages filled—
Conquest of words—
Weary eyes agreed on a truce—

Time to rest

Reason said.
Appease that beating in your breast
Drop the pen—
For Wind has blown your name
A hundred times today

Do not drown in ink
Do not let White and Blue
Chase all life away!
Smell my breath—
It's made of flowers, promises
That only I possess—

I watch the years
like an eagle watches the earth—
and I forget
often
that life
sometimes
is a mouse
walking the dirt—

age:

Always more recognition
Always more eyes
Always more craving
For fictional bonds and ties—

loneliness will eat us alive
The shy the true the distant
The ones with hearts of hope
Are patient leftovers
In the snow

The woods call me
The books call me
The ink—

This is
Survival instinct

There will always be ink
Always, always
There will always be pages

There will always be books
Always, always
There will always be the Brontës—

GLIMPSE

It's as if
the winds
the gods
had taught me to miss her
they couldn't
hold me back
from loving her
so they reached
for me
and whispered
lessons
that I now see—

I'd spread rose petals before you

But you chose to step on thorns
Barefoot—

I woke up at four with
twenty pounds of flesh-love
in my ribcage—
I wondered if
dissolving that weight involved
new eyes
or if
someone somewhere
had planned it to be
a solitary task for me—

peace or waste

I'm convinced
We could have been
A full moon—*an eclipse*—

Had we fallen
In the same time zone—

Words are my friends
They're stickers stuck on my feelings
Comforting elves
Taking primary emotions
In their arms.

When I felt better
And started to sing
I realized—

I hadn' t used my voice in months

And had forgotten

The stroke of music

My heart was
in mourning
for a golden-skinned girl's care—
as cold
as the hailstones
slapping our cheeks
and ruining our hair
that day—

But you
were the water beneath
as soft and warm
as a long-awaited bath—

Was it memories of
childhood
long-distance
innocence
reconnection
to what's been lost
taken from us
that made me
laugh
and glitter
when
we three
ran in the rain—

Or was it
the remembrance

of a thick, old bond
that I had somewhat forgotten about—

Sisters
I could run the world
if it made me hear
our endless laughters—

the Christian—

It isn't right.
It isn't God's word.

Oh, then forgive me, Lord
for I love her more than I love You—

You have been taught to me I gained You after
many lessons—

While the air separating me from her
heart felt
like a limb
I had never noticed before—

and she appeared to me when
You never had.
She was real.

I could hear her voice and touch her flesh—
You
never showed yourself

Pardon my treason; reward my honesty with your
forgiveness.

Yet I do not fear
Your judgement

isn't *Love*
Your one true word?

A blurry picture
Smoke

I'm in that in-between thing
that feels so confusing and yet
so familiar and—*double*
it can only be
human
I'm on my way back to
human living again—

It's so weird—
People are so deep

We're giants—

emotional

My heart is—

A peeled onion

My body's been
Honoured
Loved—

Slapped away—

I'm flickering
Capsizing
I'm getting *seAsiCK*

Of not knowing
Whether I want to

Throw myself at your feet
Tempt you with slow and divine kisses

or

Make my pride burn back to life
And let you deal with the wind.

I won't fall like this fallen tree
I will not let myself fall
I will remain
Strong and wild and deep—
I will not hold on to you
Because you told me not to
Because my mother and best friend said so too
Because I won't

I'll walk you out of me
I'll write you out of me
Like a medicine of air and ink.

Nature absorbs
Nature heals
Nature listens
and sings—

Nature is
A multiple friend
With an ear
Nature soothes
What's under skinned—

She clings to me
I told my diary
She sings dances whispers taunts me
Will not let me be—

And yet
I can feel her vanish
Silently leave my chest
The pain I feel for her suffering
For the first time is at rest.

It is not that I accept
It is not that I regret
It is that time has passed
Ordered the mass
Of dreams to let me rest

It's that my heart is beginning
To dissolve a haunting weight
Perhaps this is *healing*—

I have prayed for it, diary
I've written, hoped and sung—
So why can't I say farewell
Let go of a tormenting hand?

Now that the lender of painful love is standing
on the threshold of my breast
I wonder
Do I want to give it all back to him?

Do I want to say farewell?
To abandon visions and memories
Her last pieces that I have left—

let go

Your Choice Is What Matters—

Accept
that the first time
you dropped your heart
and lips
on someone else's
was
life-rising
for yourself
only—

I let
the wing of my mind
and the wing of my heart
fly
in unison:

I believed you
could be the one—
Mind and heart
in crimson—

But I'll learn to sew
mend the wings
and keep what you called purity
for someone who'll want me
I'll keep
innocence, candour, hope and my loads of
bleeding, beating flesh
for the one
who'll want me?

For them I'll be ready—

G
N
I
S
I
R

floating

s
i
n
k
i
n
g
-

My heart doesn't seem to know
What it's doing—

torrent

Over feeling,
Overthinking,
Overcontrolling
Overasking
Overgiving
Overneeding
Overexpecting
Overbleeding
Overlove.

My brain
is a rock
floating in
an ocean of
jellyfish.

overthinking

My seventy-year-old self
carries a gun
shoots my thoughts for me.

Thoughts are always accompanied
By the quickest pen
The driest movements of the hand—

I envy the butterflies
Who lives one day only
Do they really
Have reasons to overthink
To overworry—

I'm a century-old oak tree

as
branches
thoughts
with

and

a

shower

of

questions

falling on my tips—

Still need to think of her to find

some words to say—

She has lived tens of lives

She gives them everything
EVERYTHING
and everything—

She lets her being melt in their living warmth—

And when they leave
it's a process
a clock ticking back to Womb
to bring all the pieces back
together again
to be a whole again
to find herself
again.

—*the lover*

I live la vie en rose
For women are everywhere.
They teach they make me grow
And they make me despair.

to love women

amazed—

Can't you see the affliction in her eyes
Her pain—
How she learned to get heard—
And look at how she carries it
With her unutterable woman's power—

This isn't my history
The one you tell
The one you taught me
The one of
Kings, emperors
With white hands full of
Crowns—and
Whips—

My history's got colours
Waves
And hips
Its music is the cry of women giving birth
Scratching quills
And hot wind in the desert—

My history is the one behind the door
The whisper
Young children are
Never taught.

You can't break us, for we
Step on rainbows—

We have toiled to know
Who our hearts beat for

We share year-long quests
You couldn't ever know

You can't break us, for we
Step on rainbows—

Let me bare the bodies
Smell the rotting flesh
Let out the demon locked in
Scratch the skin and bones with my nails—till

Truth
Truth
The core of truth
Mask less truth
Painful, disturbing, unwanted truth

Let's her light guide me
To her simple bed so I
Can reach it
With toil, tears and the promise to let it fly
All free—

We are made
of what we read

An ancestor's machine
squeezing
the pure white linen—dripping
on the cobbles—

It is me witnessing
my love
getting a bit drier each month

It is me hoping
my love
will get a bit weaker this month.

I love this in-between moment
When the sky seems to hesitate
Between light and darkness
Pink or blue or grey
Between night and day
Though it always yields to the same choice—

black

She carries her sacrifices as
scars
hiding
in the deepest tombs of her eyes—

Woman

Confining a woman
is like
absorbing air
from Liberty
is like
drying out
an entire sea

Confining a woman
is like
depriving humanity
from
Humanity.

Knelt on the ground
dirt on her skirt
—insolent, blinding sun—
facing
the deep-dug hole
she
almost
threw herself onto

the dearest coffin—

widow.

It is their books that shaped me
built me
I
dissolved them in my blood
they' re in every cell of my body

c. e. a.

I reach you miss you look for you
struggle with you
push you away
escape ignore insult you
love you worship your
gifts—
solitude

Your first love teaches you
what you want to do to the
others who'll come
with their bodies
and cover the hole
the first left open to bleed—

I hold on to you
Friends—books and ink—
I hold on to you like
A desperate, thirsty, famished
Ghoul—

Feed your child with love
with strokes, kisses, long- embraces

So they don't beg for someone's arms
some day

So they don't look for love
where there is none to be given away—

I am in love with all women
for I love *strength—*
and I was born from one
raised by one
taught by several
led and helped
by all female breaths
brushing my skin—

Is it courage—or insanity?
to open up your chest

let the Unknown in

or the potential enemy—

They are always
SHOCKED
by words that marinate.

Point to me the one who said
we are weak—
For how could he not see
struggles
resilience
love
strength
passion
and *unconditionality*—

We are the peak of humanity.

growing

 still
But

No more petals

Like a daisy

When they shaved her head she was

If support was tangible
I'd give you bricks to build
Up stairs for you sisters

I'm standing on some northern shore—

Is it the wind?

the light

the shy, advancing waves—

The water seems to breathe—

There were a billion stars in my head

A billion never-sleeping
dragonflies—

I had never been so much awake—

My eyes
had never been—

so open—

testimony: first love memories

Ten-year-old body
budding me:

Some eyes did feel
like drops of blood
on your brand-new skin—

I thought that I was weird
but it was just the art
dancing
in my soul—

Don't forget to
Be young—

GLOW

Maybe
believing in God
requires having felt
powerless
at least once
in your life

Maybe
it's not as senseless
or weak
as I thought
Maybe
it's about
being strong

Maybe
it's being strong to
recognize
you have been
and are
powerless—

Maybe
it's courage
to reach for
help and
believe.

It's when you've lacked something that you can put a price tag on it

honesty

My best friend said
I was a fucking
FIRST CHOICE.

ballad

I shall always find my path
and
I shall always find a way
and
I shall always stand back up
to
breathe another day

I shall always meet the sun
and
the hope that comes with it
and
I shall always be grateful
for
the strength given me on a fine June day

I shall always love with mind
and
heart and eyes and rage
and
I shall always be willing
to
give myself away

But I shall always find a cure
and
remember who I am
and
remember who raised me
to
never look away

I shall always climb that wall
and
fall and climb again
and
I shall always be my own guide
and
I won't regret a day

The day that I lost Gold
I lost my world—

The day I let her go
I lost my words—

I had never felt so
Superhuman
When I was the most
Human—

When I was in love—

A caress made of silk
A sigh made of veils
And warmth—
This is how you
Should let the people you love go—

I wonder
what a relationship without
obsession
questionings
doubts
disillusioned hopes
and no risk of getting drained
or rising guilt—
feels like
what a true
honest
full
person's embrace—
what a
peaceful
healthy
mutual
blooming
love
looks like

E. J. B. —

I recognized her severity
A sister's tone in me—

Books

never betray.

It's like a machine
rolling your guts

A never-ending roll of
feelings
rising up old
emotions—

And it's like
a firework of
words
in your head—

Writing is an awakening.
An awakening of your entire being

I was told my belly
was made to bear
my hips
to give

I was told my hands were made to soothe
someone else's skin
I was told my lips
were meant to kiss

I was told to wait to speak my mind
I was taught respect

to look pretty on wedding days
to wait for mine with a prince or knight—

I took my time to learn:

my belly was made to sustain *me*
my hips ride
my hands bang a fist on the table
and write
my lips form the words I have in mind
and speak louder than my male neighbour
for whom respect is not so clear
to fix a tie around my neck
and stare at princes and princesses.

Anger:

Balls of fire

BEATING

in my arms and legs!

A body made of marble.

Then

A kick in the stomach
Urging

To run and face the foe—

                                        Fear

They prize a resurrection
but they forget
we keep rising from the dead—
we do each time
we choose to
live
while our hearts are weeping
shedding crimson tears
—we are surviving phoenixes.

Human relationships
are
Twisted
Giant tree branches

Human relationships
are
Weaved carpets, wicker baskets
Little children's braided hair.

Human relationships
are
Silver threads—
They grow hard and thick
And nothing can break them
Until
They get slack and weak
Or
Explore
Into two distorted pieces
A giant hand had welded—

But branches grow
Fingers stretch
And hair is braided differently—

And silver threads seem to grow
Independently
Before joining themselves again
For all eternity.

I couldn't see the chains couldn't guess I
could've seen the jailer in the mirror
couldn't know the threads in my head were lies:
Spiders had invaded the webs—

One day I realised—*champagne cork pop*—
A mental, wooden door squeaked to let me out—

I finally uttered the word: it was a word of love
Self-love
And freedom
One day I met a girl
An artist—for she used her skin to gild my life—
And I'm so slow I didn't realize she was opening wide
Squeaking mental, wooden doors
For me—
Draughts everywhere—

I rushed out followed her on the path of joy—
and intimacy—
I learned to speak as—she opened my mouth
Blowing her air into me—and

Songs came out
Flowing

It's only when she vanished leaving my mouth
wide open my lips unkissed that
I felt
She had murdered the jailer
Unchained the prisoner
Teaching shared desire—

I don't regret I let her go with silky caresses.

There are things we cannot say to them.
Sit down, think and see
That I'm the one who's right
There is no other way
Not wisted path—no choice to make
Nothing
To explain.

I care for you, dearest

But I will not enter your world of lies
Taboo secrets narrowmindedness
Fear shame whispers judgement
Ignorance embarrassment
Social convention religion used as destruction
Unnatural mental prison.

I will not hide—deny
Play the criminal on the run
Distort a wish to learn—

I will be shocking
Perhaps
But right and true and free.

standoff.

I am not quiet.
I am a roar you cannot hear.

Inner roars whisper
We understand fear.
What we don't understand
is the step back.

Men taught me to mistrust
Men taught me to escape
Men taught me to shut my mouth
Fear, disgust and shame

Women taught me how to read
Women taught me how to write
Women taught me how to care
Love
And shout—

Women taught me strength
Endurance
And pride.

My heart is full and deep
and it's humanity—
and if humanity
is so full and deep
then there is hope for you—and me.

Inner beauty is

A veil
An aura
An air—a colour.

I've come to realise:

First loves never erase.

First
loves
remain
clouds

Floating in the air

My heart belongs to the tormented
To the whores
The tired the weak
To the poisonous thorns
Grown out of beaten
Kids
To the lonely artists
To the musician in the street
To the ones whose alarm clocks ring at four—

For they endure
And their courage
Is the light I see when?
I feel strong no more—

First loves are
bubbles that
never explode—
they float
under—on—above
the waters of your flesh—

Something true

ecstatic

close to the human core

and ephemerality

in one-summer passions—

Make sure
when you go
that the ones you met, greeted, loved, let go
say

That one had eyes
for she could see people—

Maybe that frustration lying
in a crook of your belly
is wrong
Maybe you should stop wandering
obsessing
questioning and reviving
Maybe you should let her go
—*for she isn't coming back*—

Maybe your task was
to bring her
what you brought her
Maybe your mission is
accomplished—

You beheld my thin wrists
Heard my timid voice
Mistook me for a bird
Kissed my gentle lips

Once the time to hurt me came
Second thoughts invaded
Your endlessly-loved brain—

But you were so bewitched
By my glass-looking frame
That you forgot to check
The lion and its roar
Your chance, *your* gold—your shame.

I returned to the *sacred place*
—the first one—
I saw
others dancing and flying like you do when
you play basketball—

I recognized the familiar leaps, the steps
the imperious bounce of the ball—

And it hurt a bit
and it drew pictures I didn't want to see
and it felt like
past and present were intermingling—*viciously*—
dancing a dizzying waltz before me—
like nothing—kind of—
had happened—

But I kept my seat
and even entered the field
And after a while—
I breathed
and remembered
it had been my spot before being ours
and I decided
it shall stay my spot after being ours.

I caught a glimpse of
HOPE
and orchestrated the dance—

I saw the future
and believed
—for once—
in ballet I could lead—

I think I know
now—
Happiness lies in
hides in
stability—

Two broken hearts
make one—

A year ago I made
Someone out of ink—

If I write them less it is
A silent spell
To spare
Their wings—

She was my plane ticket to the World.

I' ll be my own flight

And destination.

optimism

Is it to trust life
Enjoy the good things only
Or is it—

To leave tomorrow in the dark
And the dark for tomorrow—

I've heard
Love is not a game.
Well sometimes it feels
Like a violent video one where
You fight
Get shot
Where your heart is offered a second or seventh life
And you must run militarily
With your wounds open and your weapons on your back
Run
In the end to save
Your ultimate life—

Smells travel
Till one of us says no
Plants the sign

STOP

Smells freeze

Get lost in the breeze—

Now I'm scared—

I feel
we lose something each time we break
—*a piece*—
leave it to the being who defined
intimacy—

and then

perhaps we end up empty
a bit more empty
with a deeper hole
for the next one to fill—

a greater
responsibility...

I desperately wanted to try
But now that I've tasted
Love
twice
I see
Innocence—the veil of innocence—
Has steamed away—

Twice my heart broke. Twice I fell. Twice I hoped and was let down.
Flew too high, got out of human reach—

Yet a billion times I will repeat
I'll follow my heart blindly.

Children find shadows frightening
But the one behind me
This shadow of a dancing tree
Is my only companion today

My body is a knot
of emotions
loss of
intimacy

I've been lied to
love isn't a gift
love is a curse
it breaks you apart
tramples your loving heart
love has no respect
and love questions time
the time they take
to go back
to the supermarket
for love in their eyes
is made of items
and you innocent babe
are just one of them
just one cheap item
back on its shelf
love is a curse
for it spoils disenchants you
love
in a word
has nothing to do with
Love
with your Disney-like idea of
Love

love
is a lie
love
is a curse
love can't be found in hearts
love is made of fists
that punch
and make your chest look black
feel sore
different
after the month they said
they're going back
to the supermarket

Be sure
I'll know when you come
for I've mastered the art
of feeling what you feel—
Be sure
I'll be in every short breath
you'll take
in every drop of sweat
every drop
of tenderness
between your legs—
Be sure
I'll be
sighing in your bed
each time you'll want to lay.
ghost

Bullet-proof vests
uniforms
guns
all on
all out—

I've entered a battlefield
naked
a child amid the bombings

But now I see
enemies—

Love is War.

I was a witch
cast a spell on our beginnings
I've lost my tricks
move my hands move my lips
but no sound of magic
can spare me
from the images
I see
you
on and in
a darker body

you
forgetting me.

Breathless to be
Powerless to be
Unable to prevent

The best for you
The worst for me—

I don't know her
Yet I do
For I know what you like.

Don't know her face
Yet I do
For I know
Your tastes

I don't know
What you'll do to her
Yet I do
For you did those things to me
I know what you like to do
To see

And she too
Will know your scent
The one between your legs
She too will know
What do you sound like when you
Come
How you close your eyes
And open your mouth—

And maybe she'll kiss
The corner of it too
Maybe she too will know
How to worship you—

Forgive me the future
stranger—unknown piece of mine
if I don't come to you with the open chest that
I once had
if I
count time
stare at the clock
before
staring at your eyes

Forgive my scars
the torment the
half-ready soul of mine
my heart will be
second-hand
and some bits you'll find lost in the wild

Forgive my childish fear that one night
I whisper words of worry

I'm not brand new you see
I'm an item some
have brought back to the store

Will you be patient future half?
with the damaged parts of mine—

My chest's no end no bottom
My chest's as large as deep as wild
As the Pacific—

Some fish have entered it
Nibbling bits of its core—my precious coral

Writing is learning
over and over again
how to breathe.

Human hearts are zombies.
They rise from the dead
And want to live.

the tombstone of heartbreak

An athletic effort
A constant reminder
To keep my head above water
I'm a runner
I'm a swimmer
  I'm drowning—struggling
But I must remember
You're not mine any more
And I must let you go.

An athletic effort
A constant reminder
To keep my head above water
I'm a runner
I'm a swimmer
  I'm drowning—struggling
But I must remember
For my own sake this time
I must let you go.

An athletic effort
A constant reminder
To keep my head above water
I'm a runner
I'm a swimmer
I'm drowning—struggling
But I must remember
I must remember.
I must remember.
I must remember.

Nothing hurts like love.
Nothing heals like love
 again—

Peace doesn't come to you
It's something you grab—

Remember what makes *you* now—
Summer that's waiting outside
Cherries growing on high, thick trees
Sleeping in the sun
And childhood memories—

Delicate postcards stories
The old lady next door
Who speaks to her cat out loud?
Playing hide and seek
With your baby cousins—

For peace doesn't come to you
It's something you grab
It's something you decide
So everything can be all right.

You think that nature helps
that other
colours
odours
do—
You think that working rests
your overthinking, your chest—

When I think that you
are the answer to it all?
for you decide to see
through your tears their waterfall—

There I come, soul mate
There I come
Wait for me
Can't you see me.
Running to you
The lives of heart-breaking are slowing me
But there I come, soul mate
Wait for me

A Year has Passed

I've found the same seat on my parents' threshold
The same roses around me
calmly seated
calmly growing
caring for *me*—

I've found the same sun
warming my shell
gently kissing all of my pains—

A year has passed
A cycle of life—

Soothing Nature calls
again
Soothing Nature helps
forget
erase—

Lightening, gentle friend
Allow me to lie in your summer again
Lick my wounds with your burning tongue
For I am the same, yet not the same—

I've been a wild flower this year
I've grown and changed colours
I met thorny roses
That made inner daisies grow

At least when they leave
they leave
a will
to be good to yourself

―me myself and I

Summer's calling again—

Erasing every thought

Every colour of pain

The sun's calling again—

in summer
I believe in God

If I had to pray
for a god
I'd pray for
the sun
for it is
my mother my father
my lover
my nest and bed
and my peaceful reminder
that life is made of silent friends—

I am never more myself
Then when I write
Then when I love.

I found my soul in a poem

A poem found my soul

I wrote my soul away—